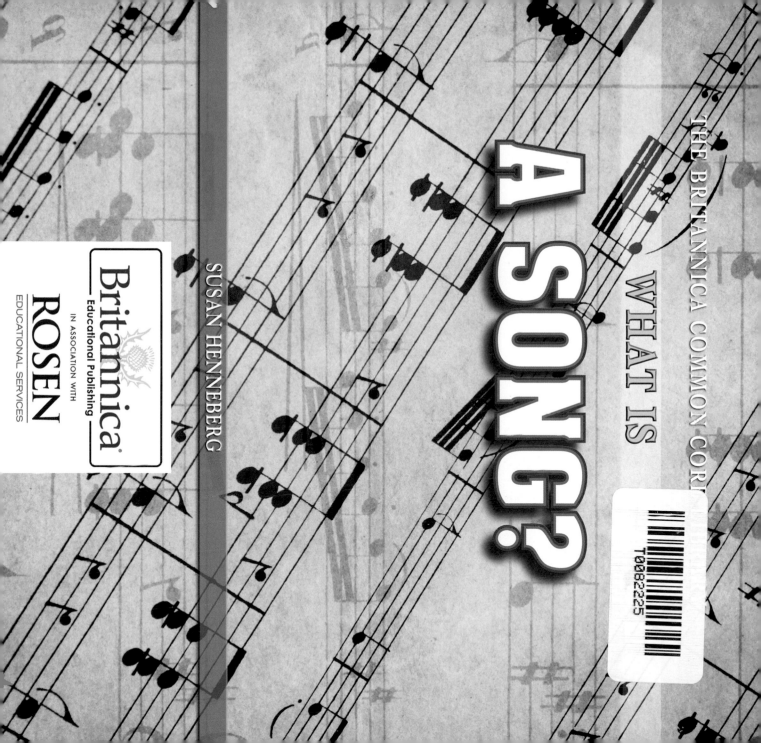

WHAT IS

A SONG?

SUSAN HENNEBERG

Britannica
Educational Publishing
IN ASSOCIATION WITH
ROSEN
EDUCATIONAL SERVICES

T0082225

Published in 2015 by Britannica Educational Publishing (a trademark of Encyclopaedia Britannica, Inc.) in association with
The Rosen Publishing Group, Inc.
29 East 21st Street, New York, NY 10010

Distributed exclusively by Rosen Publishing.
To see additional Britannica Educational Publishing titles, go to rosenpublishing.com.

First Edition

Britannica Educational Publishing
J.E. Luebering; Director, Core Reference Group
Mary Rose McCudden: Editor, Britannica Student Encyclopedia

Rosen Publishing
Hope Lourie Killcoyne: Executive Editor
Christine Poolos: Editor
Nelson Sá: Art Director
Michael Moy: Designer
Cindy Reiman: Photography Manager

Library of Congress Cataloging-in-Publication Data

Henneberg, Susan, author.
What is a song?/Susan Henneberg.
  pages cm. —(The Britannica common core library)
Includes bibliographical references and index.
ISBN 978-1-62275-664-3 (library bound) — ISBN 978-1-62275-665-0 (pbk.) — ISBN 978-1-62275-666-7 (6-pack)
1. Songs —History and criticism —Juvenile literature. I. Title.
ML2500.H46 2015
782.4209—dc23

2014013913

Manufactured in the United States of America

CONTENTS

What Is a Song?

A song is a piece of music for voices. Since ancient times, speech and music have been combined into song to express great feeling about something. Songs can be sung by one voice or by two or more voices together. Musical instruments may or may not be used to accompany, or play along with, the singing of lyrics.

There are many types of songs. Two major types are folk and art

Lyrics are the words of a song.

Students often sing different types of songs in a school choir or music class.

Taylor Swift performs pop songs for audiences. Popular music is also called pop.

songs. Folk songs are traditional songs sung by common people. They usually are learned by ear and often are not written down. The melody and words may change over time. Art songs are meant to be performed for an audience. They are more complicated than folk songs. The words and music are equally important. They do not change over time. Popular songs have developed from both folk and art songs. They are performed by professionals for an audience.

Why Do People Sing Songs?

Songs have always been a part of daily life. People sing songs to celebrate happy events or to express their feelings about sad events. They may sing spirituals or hymns to show their religious beliefs.

Protest songs help people express anger about being treated unfairly. Some workers

People often sing songs, such as "Happy Birthday to You," at birthday celebrations.

SONGWRITERS

In the 1960s, American folksinger Bob Dylan wrote songs to protest injustice and war.

create songs with a strong beat to keep their movements together. They may also create songs to pass the time during dull work. Songs can also help teach about a subject or an event. Many children learn the alphabet with a song. Parents sing lullabies, or bedtime songs, to help children go to sleep. Many songs, like playground songs at recess, are just for fun.

Babies enjoy hearing their parents sing to them.

Types of Songs

Songs can be about anything. They can also take many forms. Ballads tell a story. They can tell of relationships between people or of important events. They can also just describe a place or a feeling.

Patriotic songs express loyalty and pride. Many countries choose one patriotic song to be their national song, or anthem.

Art songs are performed for an audience, but many folk songs are sung by casual

One of the first songs that students learn to sing in school is their country's national anthem.

Patriotic means showing love of your country.

groups. In performances of folk songs, the audience may be asked to sing along. In call-and-response songs, one person sings a line and then others answer back. In rounds, a group of people sing the same song, but they don't all start at the same time. One group will start the song and then another will start after the first group.

A solo is a piece of music that is meant to be performed by just one singer or musician. The soloist may be accompanied by one or more instruments, such as the piano.

Noteworthy Songs

The following examples highlight the lyrics of some well-known songs.

"Home on the Range"

The state song of Kansas is known to most Americans. It was first written as a poem in 1873 by Dr. Brewster M. Higley after he moved to Kansas. It soon became a popular song loved by cowboys and pioneers. The original

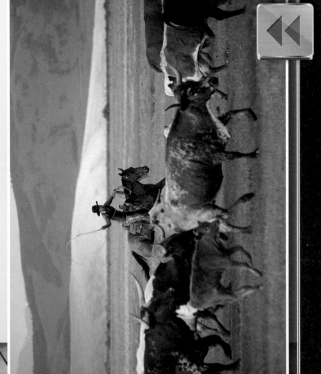

Why might cowboys have loved the song "Home on the Range"?

song is made up of six **verses** and a **chorus**. Over time, the lyrics underwent changes. It became Kansas's state song in 1947. Below is the original first verse:

Oh, give me a home where the buffalo roam,
Where the deer and the antelope play;
Where seldom is heard a **discouraging** *word*
And the sky is not cloudy all day

A **chorus** is a part of a song that repeats.

A **verse** is a part of a song that tells a story.

Discouraging means making someone less determined, hopeful, or confident.

What words in the first verse help you understand what a home on the range was like?

"Amazing Grace"

In 1772, a British man named John Newton wrote "Amazing Grace" as a poem. It is about being lifted up from despair. Newton worked in the slave trade. Eventually he joined the fight against slavery and became active in religion. He wrote his poem to express his change of heart. The hymn is well-known as both a religious song and as a song for social change. The first of

Why do you think that "Amazing Grace" is often used as a song for social change?

SONGWRITERS

Gospel music is a form of African American religious music. It can be traced back to slaves in North America in the 1700s

the song's original
six verses is below:

Amazing grace!
how sweet the
sound.
That saved a
wretch like me!
I once was lost,
but now am
found,
Was blind, but
now I see.

Small groups of singers, choirs, and soloists perform gospel music. Singers are usually very emotional and expressive.

Let's Compare

"Home on the Range" and "Amazing Grace" were both originally written as poems. Each work expresses a very personal experience that the writer had. Both songs have become very popular. Many people can connect to the words in these songs.

Yet the two songs are very different in terms of what they are describing. "Home on the Range"

Most countries have songs that describe the unique features of their land, such as snow-capped mountains.

SONGWRITERS

Bob Marley was from the island country of Jamaica in the West Indies. His songs describe the struggles and poverty of the people in the West Indies. These songs made the reggae style of music popular around the world.

celebrates the beauty of the unsettled American plains. "Amazing Grace" celebrates the strength of the human soul as it faces terrible struggles. One song describes a person's beautiful surroundings as home. The other song describes a goodness that makes a feeling of home come from inside that person.

"John Henry"

A famous work song is a ballad about John Henry. He was an African American railroad construction worker known for his strength. John Henry bet that he could drive a steel spike into solid rock as fast as a newly invented steel-driving machine could do it. Using only his hammer, he won the race and the bet but died from trying so hard. Some

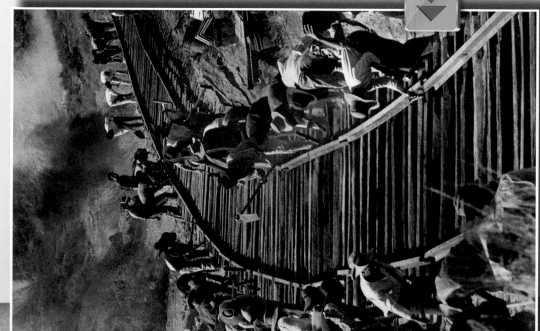

Railroad workers often created songs about the difficult job of laying tracks.

Country singer and songwriter Johnny Cash performed a famous version of "John Henry."

say he really died of a broken heart. Below is one verse of the song:

> *John Henry told his captain,*
> *"A man ain't nothin' but a man,*
> *And before I'd let your steam drill beat me down*
> *I'd die with this hammer in my hand.*
> *I'd die with my hammer in my hand."*

A statue in West Virginia was made to honor the legend of John Henry.

"Danny Boy"

Englishman Frederic Edward Weatherly wrote "Danny Boy" in 1913. The ballad was embraced by Irish people before becoming known around the world. The speaker of the song says good-bye to a beloved Danny. It is not clear where Danny will go or for how long. The speaker ends by saying that in life or death, they will meet again. Below is the first half of the song:

Frederic Weatherly wrote the words of "Danny Boy" and set them to an old Irish tune.

Oh, Danny Boy, the pipes, the pipes are calling

From glen to glen, and down the mountain side,
The summer's gone and all the roses falling;
It's you, it's you must go and I must **bide.**

But come *ye* back when summer's in the meadow,
Or when the valley's hushed and white with snow,
It's I'll be here in sunshine or in shadow,
Oh, Danny Boy, I love you, love you so!

Bide means to wait.
Ye means you.

How do the scenes described in "Danny Boy" make you feel? Why?

Let's Compare

"John Henry" and "Danny Boy" are both sad ballads. The people within each story face hardship with courage and spirit. People often feel struggles like these in their own lives. The songs help them gain strength and deal with difficulties.

John Henry shows the love and loyalty he has for his work when he says, "I'd die with my hammer in my hand." He refuses to be replaced by a machine as long as he lives. The song shows that John Henry has something a machine can never have: spirit.

Street musicians entertain their audiences by singing ballads, or folktales set to music.

SONGWRITERS

Folksinger Woody Guthrie wrote more than 1,000 songs, including "This Land Is Your Land." His songs continue to be sung casually by groups of people and performed on stage.

The lyrics in "Danny Boy" that say, "I'll be here in sunshine or in shadow," show that the speaker has great loyalty to Danny. The speaker will wait for Danny in spite of any "shadow" (or difficulty) that may come.

Guthrie arrived in New York City in the 1940s and became known as the "Oklahoma Cowboy."

"The Star-Spangled Banner"

"The Star-Spangled Banner" was written by Francis Scott Key during the War of 1812. Key watched the British attack U.S. Fort McHenry one night in 1814. At dawn, Key saw the U.S. flag still flying over the fort. It had not fallen to the British. Relieved, Key wrote a poem about the battle. After it was published, people began singing it to a popular tune. It became the national

Francis Scott Key watched the attack on Fort McHenry from a ship in the harbor.

anthem of the United States in 1931.

Here is the last part of the first verse:

And the rockets' red glare, the bombs bursting in air;
Gave proof through the night that our flag was still there:
*O say does that star-**spangled** banner yet wave,*
O'er the land of the free and the home of the brave.

Spangled means decorated.
An **anthem** is a song of loyalty, praise, or happiness.

The U.S. flag that Key saw and wrote his song about still exists. It is displayed in the Smithsonian's National Museum of American History in Washington, D.C.

"Nkosi Sikelel' iAfrika"

The title "Nkosi Sikelel' iAfrika" means "God Bless Africa." It was first sung in South African churches in the isiXhosa language. It eventually became part of the national anthem of South Africa. It is also used in Tanzania, Zambia, Namibia, and Zimbabwe. A teacher named Enoch Sontonga wrote "Nkosi Sikelel' iAfrika" in 1897 as a hymn. Seven more verses were added in 1927. In Xhosa and

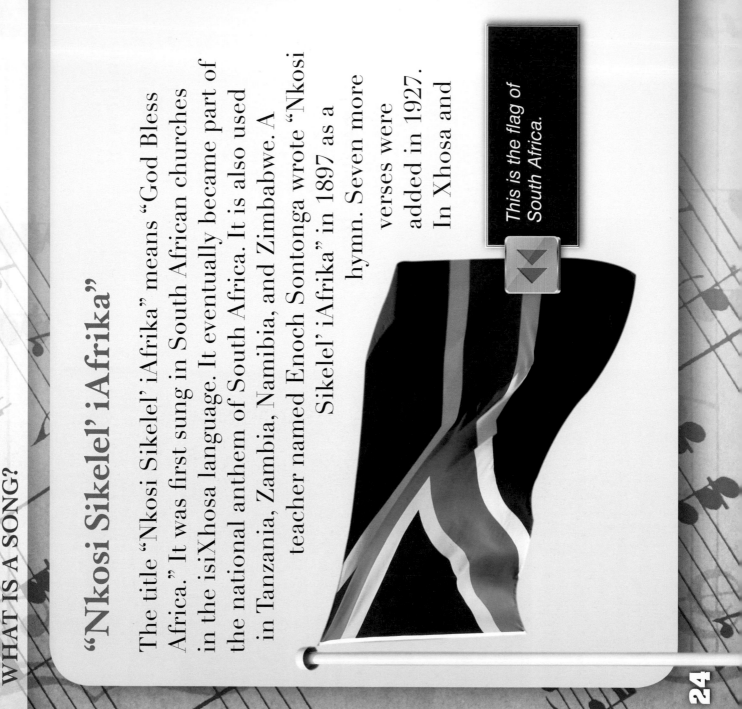

This is the flag of South Africa.

Symbols are objects that stand for something else.

Zulu culture, the "horn" mentioned below is a symbol of ancestors and power. The English translation of the original "Nkosi Sikelel' iAfrika" is:

Lord, bless Africa;
May her horn rise high up;
Hear Thou our prayers
and bless us.
Chorus
Descend, O Spirit,
Descend, O Holy Spirit.

The Zulu are a people of South Africa. For many years they have farmed grain and herded cattle.

Let's Compare

"The Star-Spangled Banner" and "Nkosi Sikelel' iAfrika" are very different national anthems in the way that they describe symbols.

"The Star-Spangled Banner" has very complicated lyrics. Many things are happening. It isn't clear if "the rockets' red glare" is coming from the enemy. However, the light it gives at night helps the speaker see "that our flag was still there." The "star-spangled banner" in the song is the symbol for the United States of America's

Olympic gold medal winners hear their national anthem played at the medal ceremony.

power as a nation to withstand an attack.

"Nkosi Sikelel' iAfrika" has very simple lyrics. The horn is a very simple symbol connected to a very old history. Many African people know the horn connects to their understanding of cattle, ancestors, and power. Power comes as the horn rises and a spirit descends.

Fans often sing the national anthem before an athletic event begins.

Write Your Own Song

Are you ready to write your own song? Here are some steps to get you started.

1. Pick your topic: Pick a topic that means a lot to you and that fills you will feeling. It can be from your own life, from nature, or from a tall tale.

2. Choose the type of song: Do you want it to be an anthem, a playground song, or a ballad? Your choice depends on what you want to say about your topic.

3. Decide what kind of tone to use: Songs can be

The notes and words of a song are written out so that other musicians can play and sing them.

sad, sweet, funny, or solemn. How do you feel about your topic? Your lyrics should reflect your feelings.

4. **Write your lyrics:** Your lyrics may or may not rhyme. You can put verses together to make a story, or ballad. You can have a chorus that repeats after every verse, or less often.

5. **Put your song to music:** You can use a melody that you find yourself humming, or use one from another song. Again, the tone of your melody should reflect your feelings.

6. **Sing it:** Sing your song to family members or friends. Or, record it so you can listen to it by yourself.

You can write a song to celebrate a special event, such as a birthday or a new family member.

Glossary

accompanied Occurred along with something.

art song A song that is written to be performed for an audience.

folk song A traditional song sung by common people and usually played by ear.

gospel music A form of African American religious music.

hymn A religious song.

lullabies Songs used to help children fall asleep.

melody The tune of a song.

popular song A song performed by professionals for an audience, often for money.

rhyme Words that have the same sounds.

rhythm A repeated pattern of sounds; a beat.

For More Information

Books

Ajmera, Maya, Elise Hofer Derstine, and Cynthia Pon. *Music Everywhere*. Watertown, MA: Charlesbridge Publishing, 2014.

Dylan, Bob. *Blowin' in the Wind*. New York, NY: Sterling Publishing Company, 2011.

Fox, Dan, and Dick Weissman. *The Great Family Songbook*. New York, NY: Black Dog & Leventhal Publishers, 2010.

Hamlisch, Marvin. *Marvin Makes Music*. New York, NY: Dial Books for Young Readers, 2012.

Lock, Deborah, ed. *Children's Book of Music*. New York, NY: DK Publishing, 2010.

Seskin, Steve. *Sing My Song: A Kid's Guide to Songwriting*. Berkeley, CA: Tricycle Press, 2008.

Websites

Because of the changing nature of Internet links, Rosen Publishing has developed an online list of websites related to the subject of this book. This site is updated regularly. Please use this link to access the list:

http://www.rosenlinks.com/BCCL/Song

Index